Elf-help for Healing from Divorce

D0805199

Elf-help for Healing from Divorce

written by
Kathryn Lankston

illustrated by
R.W. Alley

A ONE
CARING
PLACE

Abbey Press

Text © 2001 by Kathryn Lankston
Illustrations © 2001 by St. Meinrad Archabbey
Published by One Caring Place
Abbey Press
St. Meinrad, Indiana 47577

Library of Congress Catalog Number
2001093040

ISBN 0-87029-357-5

Printed in the United States of America

Foreword

Divorce is never easy, and perhaps this is why many people who have undergone a divorce liken it to a death. And it is a sort of death — an end of hopes, an end of dreams, sometimes an end of love itself.

But whereas death is understood quite readily, divorce frequently is not. Some people think one should not get upset over something he or she "chose" to do. Some people think divorced people "just haven't tried hard enough." Some people think that divorced people have no clear idea of what commitment is all about.

Elf-help for Healing from Divorce is written for anyone whose lives have been touched by divorce. Inside are 38 small ways to face the reality of divorce, and to begin the healing that needs to happen. The book helps people to realize that, although something has ended, life will continue, and can be good again.

1.

Respect yourself. You are a capable person who is facing difficult decisions and emotions. Look at yourself in the mirror each day and smile with gentle admiration and honest encouragement.

2.

Don't be ashamed. The experience of divorce does not make you a second-class citizen. Your dreams for yourself are always worthwhile—yesterday, today, and tomorrow.

3.

Consult the professionals you need. There are men and women especially trained in the emotional complexities and legal details of divorce. Talk with these people to determine who best can offer what you need during this time.

4.

Feel God's love and grace. As Max Ehrmann notes in the "Desiderata": "You are a child of the universe, no less than the trees and the stars."

5.

Don't belabor your friends
with details or demand their
advice. Let your friends support
you—but do not expect them
to be your therapist, lawyer,
or spiritual advisor.

6.

Continue to do the good things
for yourself you've always done.
You may want to make a list
of the self-care things you do—
and be sure you do at least one
each day.

7.

Grieve. The experience of loss
is not limited to physical death.
You are facing the death of
dreams you once held dear.
Respect that fact and grieve
that loss.

8.

Don't consider yourself a "failure." The feelings of pain and loss do not mean you have "failed." Rather, you chose love, day after day and through the years—and one who chooses to love is not a failure.

9.

Don't make unnecessary major decisions during this time. Apply your energy and wisdom to the pressing decisions that must be made relative to your divorce. The time will come for other major issues.

10.

Maintain trusted relationships.
Let close family members and
friends be your companions
through this unfamiliar time.
Don't isolate yourself from the
people who care about you.

11.

Don't enter a new primary relationship too soon. The years of marriage and the experience of divorce contain great depths of wisdom for you. Take your time and let your heart, mind, and soul learn all the valuable lessons your life experience has to offer.

12.

Keep your children out of the middle. Regardless of their ages, your children are experiencing an especially painful time as well. Do not add to their pain and confusion by trying to influence their affections or loyalties.

13.

Avoid "win/lose" thinking and behavior. When divorce becomes a competition, everyone loses. Consider mediation as an alternative to litigation. Focus on healing.

14.

Keep your children and loved ones informed with facts. Without the burden of details, offer your loved ones the information they need to best support you. They care.

15.

Remain especially available to your children. Regardless of their ages, your children are part of the years that have brought you to this moment. Allow your children to have and express their own emotions. No emotion is "wrong."

16.

Maintain as much of your daily routine as possible. Routine is a hidden blessing when you're dealing with so much that is unfamiliar.

17.

Concentrate on your strengths.
The many basic skills you use
in the course of your daily
routine are the primary coping
tools you can rely on during
these days and months
of change.

18.

Be alert to your weaknesses.
When we experience stress,
we often turn to bad habits
and less-than-healthy behavior,
perceiving them as means
of comfort or coping. Know
your weaknesses and avoid
their allure.

19.

Allow your faith community to support you with their prayers. You need not provide details. Just ask for the community's prayers for healing and peace.

20.

Bless all the memories of your married life—the good and the bad. All you've been through over the years holds the wisdom for the life you want to build in the future.

21.

Balance rest and activity.
You're pouring out massive
amounts of energy during this
time, so you need some measure
of extra rest. At the same time,
do not neglect your need for
basic physical activity. A daily
fifteen-minute walk can keep
you physically, emotionally,
and mentally sharp.

22.

Maintain a healthy diet. Skipping or reducing meals is never wise—nor is excessive eating. Your daily food intake provides the "fuel" you need for each day. Eat balanced meals as part of your balanced life.

23.

Don't expect too much of yourself. This is no time to prove your physical stamina or mental prowess. You don't need to be a "super" anything during this time. Just be your best self.

24.

Avoid all extremes. If you try to force too much into life or try to absorb too much from it, you lose a sense of perspective—and without a good sense of perspective, good planning for your future is at risk.

25.

Befriend change. Don't view change as threatening— for only through the cycles of change can new growth be realized. Consider the seasons; even winter gives way to spring.

26.

Let holiday traditions become something different. After all, the definition of "family" is changing for you—and thus will your "family" traditions. Give yourself and your family time to discover what needs to change—and what needs to be retained.

27.

Review your priorities—they may be shifting. Changes in a primary relationship cause ripple effects, like the ripples in a pond when a stone is cast in. Continue to ask yourself what's important now, and allow yourself different answers over the weeks and months ahead.

28.

Ritualize the removal of special mementoes from your life. Even if you don't want to save things like your wedding ring, significant photos, or other memorabilia, think carefully about what to do with them. These items were important to you at one time; what you do with them now should respect the value they once represented.

29.

Make simple changes that are yours to make. Some things <u>must</u> change; other changes can be chosen. Rearranging the furniture in your bedroom, for example, or finding a different favorite restaurant can help you make simple changes in simple ways.

30.

Seek healthy humor. Laughter is known to decrease stress by increasing the flow of oxygen in the bloodstream. Laugh often—for your own good.

31.

Rely on spiritual practices that have nurtured your spirit in the past. Scripture reading, meditation, and prayer: These practices are sources of sustenance for now and in the future.

32.

Do not try to "win over" people to "your side." This time is painful and confusing for your family and friends. Do not make it more so by campaigning for your "cause."

33.

Deal with your emotions in healthy ways. Anger, betrayal, relief, joy: Whatever your emotional experience, express yourself in ways that respect your body, mind, and spirit—and that of others.

34.

Know your own limits and respect them. Some of the responsibilities you shared as a couple may now fall to you alone. Be willing to let some things go, learn how to do new things, and ask for help when you need it.

35.

Ritualize the date of your final divorce. Just as you noted and remembered your wedding day, respectfully note and remember the date of your divorce. It's the end and the beginning of many things for you.

36.

Present yourself with a "Citation of Wisdom." List the lessons of the heart you learned during the years of your marriage. These lessons will serve as guideposts for the future.

37.

Claim your divorce. This is your experience; it is part of your life story. Using language like "my divorce" rather than "the divorce" helps you personalize this experience and foster healing.

38.

Seek a little solitude each day. Even if this is not part of your daily routine, take the time to enter the peace of stillness, where you'll find a wellspring of inner strength.

Kathryn Lankston is a free-lance author and editor with twenty years experience in publishing. She is the mother of six children from her first marriage.

Illustrator for the Abbey Press Elf-help Books, **R.W. Alley** also illustrates and writes children's books. He lives in Barrington, Rhode Island, with his wife, daughter, and son.

The Story of the Abbey Press Elves

The engaging figures that populate the Abbey Press "elf-help" line of publications and products first appeared in 1987 on the pages of a small self-help book called *Be-good-to-yourself Therapy*. Shaped by the publishing staff's vision and defined in R.W. Alley's inventive illustrations, they lived out author Cherry Hartman's gentle, self-nurturing advice with charm, poignancy, and humor.

Reader response was so enthusiastic that more Elf-help Books were soon under way, a still-growing series that has inspired a line of related gift products.

The especially endearing character featured in the early books—sporting a cap with a mood-changing candle in its peak—has since been joined by a spirited female elf with flowers in her hair.

These two exuberant, sensitive, resourceful, kindhearted, lovable sprites, along with their lively elfin community, reveal what's truly important as they offer messages of joy and wonder, playfulness and co-creation, wholeness and serenity, the miracle of life and the mystery of God's love.

With wisdom and whimsy, these little creatures with long noses demonstrate the elf-help way to a rich and fulfilling life.

Elf-help Books

...adding "a little character" and a lot
of help to self-help reading!

Teacher Therapy	#20145
Be-good-to-your-family Therapy	#20154
Stress Therapy	#20153
Making-sense-out-of-suffering Therapy	#20156
Get Well Therapy	#20157
Anger Therapy	#20127
Caregiver Therapy	#20164
Self-esteem Therapy	#20165
Take-charge-of-your-life Therapy	#20168
Work Therapy	#20166
Everyday-courage Therapy	#20167
Peace Therapy	#20176
Friendship Therapy	#20174
Christmas Therapy (color edition) $5.95	#20175
Grief Therapy	#20178
Happy Birthday Therapy	#20181
Forgiveness Therapy	#20184
Keep-life-simple Therapy	#20185
Celebrate-your-womanhood Therapy	#20189

Acceptance Therapy (color edition) $5.95   #20182

Acceptance Therapy   #20190

Keeping-up-your-spirits Therapy   #20195

Play Therapy   #20200

Slow-down Therapy   #20203

One-day-at-a-time Therapy   #20204

Prayer Therapy   #20206

Be-good-to-your-marriage Therapy   #20205

Be-good-to-yourself Therapy   #20196
   (hardcover) $10.95

Be-good-to-yourself Therapy   #20255

Book price is $4.95 unless otherwise noted.
Available at your favorite giftshop or bookstore—
or directly from One Caring Place, Abbey Press
Publications, St. Meinrad, IN 47577.
Or call 1-800-325-2511.